F L O U R I S H

FLOURISH

JACQUELINE TURNER

A MISFIT BOOK

Copyright © Jacqueline Turner, 2019

Published by ECW Press
665 Gerrard Street East
Toronto, Ontario, Canada, M4M 1Y2
416-694-3348 / info@ecwpress.com

Purchase the print edition and receive the eBook free. For details, go to ecwpress.com/eBook.

All rights reserved. No part of this publication may be reproduced, stored in a retrieval system, or transmitted in any form by any process — electronic, mechanical, photocopying, recording, or otherwise — without the prior written permission of the copyright owners and ECW Press. The scanning, uploading, and distribution of this book via the Internet or via any other means without the permission of the publisher is illegal and punishable by law. Please purchase only authorized electronic editions, and do not participate in or encourage electronic piracy of copyrighted materials. Your support of the author's rights is appreciated.

LIBRARY AND ARCHIVES CANADA CATALOGUING IN PUBLICATION

Title: Flourish / Jacqueline Turner.

Names: Turner, Jacqueline, 1965– author.

Description: Poems.

Identifiers: Canadiana (print) 2019010984X | Canadiana (ebook) 20190109955 |

ISBN 9781770415065 (softcover)
ISBN 9781773053950 (PDF)
ISBN 9781773053943 (EPUB)

Classification: LCC PS8589.U7476 F56 2019 | DDC C811/.6—dc23

Editor for the Press: Michael Holmes / a misFit Book
Cover design: Rachel Ironstone
Cover and interior artwork © Lacy Martin / www.lacymartindesign.com
Author photograph: © Len Grinke

The publication of *Flourish* has been generously supported by the Canada Council for the Arts which last year invested $153 million to bring the arts to Canadians throughout the country and is funded in part by the Government of Canada. *Nous remercions le Conseil des arts du Canada de son soutien. L'an dernier, le Conseil a investi 153 millions de dollars pour mettre de l'art dans la vie des Canadiennes et des Canadiens de tout le pays. Ce livre est financé en partie par le gouvernement du Canada.* We acknowledge the support of the Ontario Arts Council (OAC), an agency of the Government of Ontario, which last year funded 1,737 individual artists and 1,095 organizations in 223 communities across Ontario for a total of $52.1 million. We also acknowledge the contribution of the Government of Ontario through the Ontario Book Publishing Tax Credit, and through Ontario Creates for the marketing of this book.

PRINTED AND BOUND IN CANADA   PRINTING: COACH HOUSE   5 4 3 2 1

for Jack William Turner
1931–2017

CONTENTS

FLOURISH: STUDIES	13
Beauty will no longer be forbidden	15
Lost in Translation	16
The Inbetweenists	17
Buttons and Pockets	18
Una Habitación Propia	19
Lorca's Piano	20
Centro José Guerrero	21
Dear Madrid	22
Façadism	23
La Lectura	24
Tout Va Bien	25
Sketch of the Poem of Cordoba	26
Hullo, Hullo . . . ,	27
La Vega	28
Chicken or Egg	29
Tokyo Cool	30
Masterpieces	31
Love Poem for Dangerous Women	32
An H in the Heart	33
You Don't Know How Lovely You Are	34
I'd rather be reading	35
Speaking in Paragraphs	36
Tentacular Thinking	37
The Art Show	38
Zu verschenken	39
Unfurl	40

Yet	41
Eileen Myles	42
Furious	43
Something Quite Peculiar	44
Placebo Effect	45

NEW NOSTALGIA   47

What's the matter with you	49
Distrust	50
New York Intellectuals	51
Video Cameras	52
Surprise!	53
Cognizant	54
Some Place	55
Anticipation and Exile	56
The Local Exile	57
Assemblages	58
Recognition Vector	59
New York Intellectuals II	60
How Does It Feel	61
Anticipating Nostalgia	62
Putting the World in a Box	63
Tender Feelings	64
Awkward Feelings	65
Awkward Writer Feelings	66
Reading	67
Mother/hood	68
Momness	69
It Was Meant to Be Simple	70

FLOURISH: POEMS

Seven-Hearted	73
"Was it you?"	75
Infinity	77
Joy?	79
"Texts against images and vice versa"	81
"Texts against images and vice versa" II	82
"To flourish is to become dangerous"	84
"Around the cave/a luscious forest flourished: alder, poplar, and scented cypress. It was full of wings."	86
". . . immaculate possibility"	88
"all flourish there, increased by rain"	90
Flourish	92
Pavilion	94
Quietly	97
The Drink	100
The Work	102
Proposals	103

FLOURISH: DECLARATIVE SENTENCES

Dear	107
Absence	108
Presence	109
Presents	110
Light Light	111
Best	112
Volute	113
Tremour	114
The book itself	115

ACKNOWLEDGEMENTS 117

NOTES 118

"Every night I cut out my heart.
But in the morning it was full again."
— *The English Patient*

"Wow, you sure know how to do love!"
— Meredith Quartermain

FLOURISH: STUDIES

"Hence the necessity to affirm the flourishes of this writing, to give form to its movement, its near and distant byways."

— Hélène Cixous,
"The Laugh of the Medusa"

Beauty will no longer be forbidden

It will be found everywhere. In the abundance of flesh within the constraints of bikinis, the crepe skin of aging hands, in creases of foreheads, the way the light hits our laugh lines. Let it alight in the stretches of skinny jeans, the lushness of mom arms, in Caesarean scars. Let us worship the crinkles of eyes, the problem skin. Let blemishes reign, let us adore the rosacea and any asymmetry. We will move through the world in whatever fits us, whatever we wish. Light gauzy fabric or a plethora of denim, caftans or crew necks, pearls or no. Flannel or overalls, rompers or suits. Let hair have no bad days, curly or straight, buzzed or piled high, pulled back or hung, tendrils flinging like snakes. Let it be grey or green or whatever we choose. Let it be shaved or waxed or plying out from panties. Let legs "gleam like petrified mammoth tusk" or riot in a hairy array, encased in yoga pants, pantyhose or not. Let nails be bare or lacquered, bitten or embossed. Let bras be comfortable or disregarded. Let freedom (finally) be the beauty factor: "In one another we will never be lacking."

Lost in Translation

In a karaoke room in Shibuya featuring all you can drink cocktails I'm trying to sing "Brass in Pocket" like Scarlett Johansson's character in *Lost in Translation*. I'm with my sons instead of Bill Murray but the comedy is similar. Gonna use my style, gonna use my substance (we substitute for sidestep) gonna use my my my imagination. I can't hit the notes and struggle to feel substantial, substantive. It's a common struggle. Recent celebrity suicides make the ethereal grasp evident. Jhumpa Lahiri's *In Other Words* says, "What does a word mean? And a life? In the end, it seems to me, the same thing. Just as a word can have many dimensions, many nuances, great complexity, so, too, can a person, a life." *Substantial* translates variously in Japanese from *juyo* (important) to *judai* (serious) to *juyona* (significant) but how to enact the feeling of substance for people, to let them know how we feel, how much they matter. "Because ultimately the meaning of a word, like that of a person, is boundless, ineffable."

The Inbetweenists

Some people are narrativists and some people are episodicists according to Julian Barnes writing about Lucian Freud and quoted in a book about time by Heidi Julavits. "Narrativists feel responsibility for their actions and guilt over their failures; episodicists think that one thing happens, and then another thing happens . . ." I'm more so an episodicist, but pose a theory that poets fit in neither category and more inhabit the space of the long dash of Emily Dickinson, the place of possibility, the moment before the leap when I want to jump from the cliff into the lucid blue ocean but can (almost) not make myself go. The posed moment of the inbetweenist. In Madrid, I see Lucian Freud's *Last Portrait* (1976–1977) and I see that moment between the real and the unreal made manifest where space is rendered for the rest of the quintessential Freudian portrait to take up and I see that it's somewhat vacant, almost blank, and I see that I can fill it with my knowledge and imagining of it based on the information being presented by what I see in the rest of the portrait. Is the woman being overtaken by the shaped blank space or is she fading from view, hovering conditionally in between her life and her eventual demise? "The distinction is existential not moral. Episodicists see and feel little connection between the different parts of their life, have a more fragmentary sense of life . . ." It's as if the psychological intensity is apparent in the body of the portrayed, the ragged brush stroke of the painter, the conception of the poet. "Happily (or confusingly), in most of us these tendencies overlap" thus inbetweenism is a substantial thing.

Buttons and Pockets

"My dress falls over my head. A shadow overtakes me," Harryette Mullen writes in *Trimmings*. Running a collaborative experiment in an art school where I ask students working in groups to make selections from a box of buttons, each taking a turn without talking with the goal of creating a button-based tableau and gaining insights into nonverbal communication, I encounter a student with a morbid fear of buttons. "It's as if you gave us a box filled with spiders," says the student. I'm skeptical but indulge the affectation. The dress I'm wearing has pockets and I jam my hands into them. Koumpounophobia is rare but does exist Google suggests when I look it up later. Have you ever seen me wearing a button, they ask, and no you have to admit they're right. Famously Neil Gaiman gave Coraline a fear of buttons, which was how this student came to realize their own fear. "Sew buttons on, but they are slow to open flowers — imagine the color," writes Mullen and I remember my mother darning dark blue socks using an old lightbulb as form. In the dark of 3 a.m. insomnia I suspect my student will hate this poem.

Una Habitación Propia

"A woman must have money and a room of her own if she is to write fiction," Virginia Woolf famously said and Andrés Soria Olmedo takes this notion and applies it to the educational life of Federico García Lorca in a show detailing the pedagogical experiment of La Residencia de Estudiantes in Granada whose interlocutors included Salvador Dalí among others. Later we have dinner with Andrés and Lisa takes a selfie with him which we all agree is fabulous. My own room in Granada is a good size with a window overlooking a tae kwon do club and two beds with bright purple comforters. I get a lot of writing done breaking open projects which have begun to haunt me. The third period of the Lorca show spanning from 1926 to 1928 "reflects the moment in which the formative efforts of the previous years yielded fruitful results on different levels and in different forms . . ." In my room, the counting from the tae kwon do club forms a metric constraint and I compress writing moments in between numbers and sky.

Lorca's Piano

Fiona asks to play Lorca's piano and the guide says, "Sí, sí." She lightly touches down and the space is transformed from monument to poetic text as music rushes around the room that is no longer an actual room. No photos allowed in the space so we just have to remember. Later I photograph another of Lorca's pianos in another of his houses, this one in Valderrubio — the only house where photo taking is allowable. The guide tells a story about the town previously being called *Asqueroso*, which he says means *disgusting* in Spanish. The guide tells us that the name was eventually changed, but in the moment being represented in the house, Lorca always assigned a different place name when writing letters to friends so as not to have to refer to it as *asqueroso*. In a letter framed in one of Lorca's bedrooms he asks his father to please buy him a piano.

Centro José Guerrero

The window frames a slice of the cathedral at the end of abstract expressionism up against Guerrero from the lateral series. The juxtaposition is pleasing so I photograph it and post it on Instagram. 8 likes. I'm tired and sit and stare at the painting for quite a while. People are waiting for me, but still. When James Elkins wrote *Pictures & Tears: A History of People Who Have Cried in Front of Paintings*, he was talking about paintings like this. Abstraction (he meant Rothko more) leaves space for emotions to rise unexpectedly. It happens in poetry maybe less often. No maybe more. Probably way more. Which is why there is not a book about the history of people who have cried in front of poems. The most interesting crying he writes about is the crying no one can understand. "Some viewers see more than they expect," he writes. Some viewers refuse to be moved. "Crying is often a mystery," he writes, "and for that matter so is not crying."

Dear Madrid

The invocation to become familiar is the welcoming gesture of the structure of travel. Stone edges kindly demarcate a view of such lustre that history rises to meet its contemporary reflections. We see again an intimacy that we have always desired. Here — on the rooftop bar — we rise up to meet ourselves again hoping to be transformed. Here — in this later space — we write ourselves a letter: dear Jacqueline(s): don't forget . . . and etc.

Façadism

A cartoon façade hides the reconstruction of Madrid City Hall in a way that is somehow more real than scaffolds and blue tarps. A clad tower (for all to see) featuring a replica on the real city hall rises to meet the clouds. Jane Jacobs writes, "Planning for vitality must aim at clarifying the visual order of cities, and it must do so by both promoting and illuminating functional order, rather than by obstructing or denying it." I see taking trouble to print a covering that looks as if it is the original city hall as a massive nod to tourism, forgetting for the moment that I am the tourist, I am the tourism. In Vancouver, an art exhibit features projections onto the façade of the gallery that used to be a courthouse. The projected colours and texts transform the rigidity of the columns underneath, reconfiguring the functional order and bringing the gallery role to the surface for once. The new art gallery in Vancouver will be modelled after an inukshuk, a symbol demonstrating a vast historical inaccuracy and covering over (once again) the unceded lands on which it will sit.

La Lectura

We like reading more than writing. Would spend our days on divan or chaise lounge surrounded by books and velvet curtains, propped on stacks of pillows. Reading is a space that makes multiple lines of thought emerge or reading is a space to follow someone else's thought so thoroughly we can quiet our own. In an interview Karl Ove Knausgaard says, "When I figured out that writing is just like reading then I could write again." We are not sure what this means, which is perhaps why we are not novelists or relentlessly detailed memoirists. Reading is expansive and reading is crunching down on the details. Reading is riding the narrative or imbibing the syllables. Meaning resides with us, precious readers.

Tout Va Bien

In situ commes des garçons, a temporal utopia. We'll shift it if we can to reveal an affective economy making emotional linkages in the production of fear as if all can go well. Alignments are not even subtle but still we might try to see what surfaces always reveal. A certain whiteness, discrediting a witness, all those colonial names. Missing women. So many. If in a skiff on the Salish Sea or riding out the narcissism of a nation or the subtext of a speech bubble. Crunching the delineations of woke banshees everywhere and our famous detractors who shut us up in the guise of loyalty. The contemporary moment is so blunt. All goes for sure.

Sketch of the Poem of Cordoba

The symbolic value of seven women is wrenched through layers of historical lenses. Materiality of paint sculpts the poem's form and attracts me via the poem in its title. I talk about poetry and painting all the time, saying things in classrooms like, "If this painting wasn't a painting but a poem, what would it be?" Meaning each are languages, meaning paint can be poem-like and vice versa. Meaning, try translating the gesture from form to form in order for thinking to be generative. Etel Adnan writes, "Furiously, I became a painter. I immersed myself in that new language." This sketch of a poem painting shows the desire to articulate place in a nuanced way to maybe push past the limits of symbolism to generate a multiplicity of meanings and to inhabit an ambiguity that symbolism belies. I take a non-flashing photograph, buy the postcard as I exit through the gift shop, think about writing a poem in response to the painting later.

Hullo, Hullo . . . ,

The leaps Rose Wylie makes into encapsulating the everyday onto large scale canvases strike me as impactful in her bold colour alignments of the news with little regard for classical considerations. At the age of 76 she made the *Women to Watch* exhibition, which makes her an emerging-mid-career-late-career hybrid in the way that Lynne Tillman talks about Etel Adnan a "Lebanese-born painter and poet who is 92. About six years ago, *she* was 'discovered' and now can't keep up with the demand for her work. The work of both painters feels incredibly contemporary and heroic in dispelling ageist assumptions but their alignment with the literary is what strikes me the second time. Wylie's paintings are 'open-end stories' and Adnan's 'vivid, abstract paintings explore seeing, being.'" The third time I'm struck is in my selfish realization that I am beyond mid-career and my poetic work (abstract and open-ended) has yet to be alighted upon. "Hullo, Hullo, Following-on After the News" (2017) and etc.

La Vega

Lush produce results from the labour of migrant farm workers and these habas con jamón arrive on the plate at La Tana where the late Anthony Bourdain did an episode of his show in Granada via their efforts. We join the 8:30 lineup several nights to be the first in the door and get a good seat at the bar. The owner Jesus pours wine by the glass letting everyone taste first. Spain hires 7,000 seasonal female farm workers from Morocco. The morning ritual of tostado con tomates at Los Pensadores is also thanks to their invisible hands. Skin cells linger. We are who we eat.

Chicken or Egg

A chicken is just an egg's way of getting another egg is a thing I heard on a podcast recently. I have (jokingly) imagined curating whole classes based on the application of particular podcasts or conducting therapy via podcast recommendations. So much of what we do is applying the things we've heard to the appropriate contexts so this is merely expanding the range of usefulness. I feel the cellular connection to my own offspring in the world and can conceptualize containing their cells for all eternity too. Bodies are finite obviously but perpetual too. What would last or remain of women or salmon, and how ecologies become knowledgeable are only a couple of ways to think about it in the transfer of nutrients alone. Googling bodies of salmon leads to stories about remains of bodies of women on a farm near the small city of Salmon Arm near where I grew up. The Pickton parallels reverberate through recent histories. Horror is perpetual too.

Tokyo Cool

The way time shifts is the most compelling element of travel. Arrive at 9 p.m. but it feels like 9 a.m. and we're just not hungry. Seeing how the body adapts to the frenetic pace of Tokyo versus the leisurely afternoon siestas in the south of Spain makes the artificial construct of time more visible. In *Moshi Moshi* Banana Yoshimoto writes of a Tokyo neighbourhood, "The way things are going, there will be less and less space for individuals to find their niche within a community, and less and less leeway for people to live at a pace that suits them." Stepping out of schedules creates a pace building self-reflective potential for new niche-finding upon the return. We might stay up later when we get back, we might not work so much but only within what the architectures of time allow. Ali Smith in *Artful* writes, "Art itself is a broken thing if it's anything, and that the act of remaking, or imagining, or imaginative involvement, is what makes the difference." We might imagine ourselves Tokyo cool, but then fall back into typical patterns almost immediately.

Masterpieces

Super famous art often looks familiar to me because of the Masterpiece board game I played as a kid. The world presented in the game, set as an art auction, was as far from my small town reality as possible. We bid up van Gogh's *Sunflowers* and coveted its win. My friend painted her VW van with sunflowers and drove across the country with her small daughter. I see a van Gogh in Madrid, *Les Vessenots in Auvers*, and think of her even though we are now estranged. There are few ways to talk about a breakup with a friend. She texts me in Granada to say she has a new phone number in Victoria and even though we're not talking she wants me to have it. I text her back to say I'm happy for her, happy, so happy. The didactic panel of the painting notes van Gogh "was prey to all manner of conflicting moods: the vast expanses of fertile cropland gave him a sense of freedom, but at the same time intensified the feeling of melancholy and loneliness." I have wondered if a progressive form of melancholy is possible but this wondering came before those divisive red hats, which use nostalgia as a hammer to mobilize an electorate around a false history of America that so patently tries to erase the America experienced by Black people. Before a Canadian government valourized its relationship with First Nations with the nostalgia of the language of reconciliation as its public inquiries were failing. Nostalgia has a lot of answer for.

Love Poem for Dangerous Women

We will in the streets, the classrooms, the boardrooms. We will on Twitter, on Facebook, in podcasts to whoever is listening. We will at readings in bookstores and libraries, university campuses and college benches. We will in high schools. We will in galleries and studios, garrets and ivory towers. We will on buses and trains, in cars, on planes and boats of every description. We will in plazas and commons, parks and beaches. We will in bars, and restaurants, and whatever coffee shops. We will in back alleys late at night and park benches at dawn. We will by statues, graffiti, public art, and community gardens. We will.

An H in the Heart

I stumble upon *Strang* by Roy Kiyooka at the AGO, having been forced out of an expensive Airbnb near the CN Tower with nowhere to keep my bags before the evening flight. The coat check attendant happily takes my $4 and I am unemcumbered as I move through the nooks and wood adorned hallways and small rooms. Group of Seven this and Emily Carr that. After posting a photo to Instagram linking to the account "An H in the Heart," which features artful *H*s everywhere, poet Cam Scott replies, "Oh that's great! I know some of the more symmetrical paintings, which remind me of how bpNichol talks about *H* as containing a bridge between two isolated egos; I think that in Kiyooka's bridge paintings the egg-shaped auras around each stem show that abutting separateness too." Contemplating the harsh edges as bridges with the softer swoops as cellular divides and multiplies the potential meaning of the work. I wonder about the confidence of the painter (as a genre) in relation to my own desire to not talk myself out of writing poems. How to lay down the line across the unwritten to the poem itself, to make it firm with light hatches of possibility?

You Don't Know How Lovely You Are

My Twitter handle, @intothefold — taken from the title for my first book of poetry — is also the name of a style blogger (she got the Instagram name) so I often get mis-tagged in fashion posts. *Into the Fold* blog is described as "a website for young women, by young women, a universal diary of sorts," which is not that far off from my book, the back cover of which indicates, "It maps longing while exploring how the triple pull of the domestic, erotic, and geographic are enacted in a woman's life." I was a (relatively speaking) young woman at the time of writing it. *Into the Fold* is the most aesthetically fashionable of all of my books, even though yellow is rare in covers and hard to pull off. Adrian Searle writes of Gillian Wearing's *Self Portrait as My Sister Jane Wearing*, where she makes and wears masks of her relatives, "This is what we call a personal voice, which we often take for a kind of authenticity, generated by some inner spark: the essential me inside the mess of being alive." Capital F fashion masks unexpected beauty, thus there is so much, so much! you might not know about how lovely you are, how lovely it is that you are alive.

I'd rather be reading

If it's 3 a.m. I'm probably reading although I'd probably actually rather be sleeping. Reading when it's dark out mellows the senses to a fine but prismatic focus. Thoughts drift in my mind and back to the page, the story takes form and the narrative revs up its drive train or it doesn't. Sometimes I jump on and jump off, sometimes I ease back and let it carry me forward in time. I embrace the blur, my eyes droop, I refocus for a second and then drift back to the page. When I can't maintain, I run my hands along the hallway wall to the bedroom, roll onto the high bed, negotiate my way into the curve of D.'s back, lightly kiss his neck, and slowly slumber off into the soujourn of sleep.

Speaking in Paragraphs

I don't but I know people who do. Fully formed ideas fall out of their mouths with captivating hooks, building action, and a clever return back to the beginning just as they are winding down. People who verbally process their experiences do not like to be interrupted. They are likely to barrel over interjections unless I'm so uncharacteristically forceful that I can't be reasonably ignored. Their resulting exasperation is palpable enough that I almost feel bad for trying to take up space with my fragmentary hesitative speech parts. bpNichol wrote, "The mouth remembers what the brain can't quite wrap its tongue around & that's what my life's become. My life's become my mouth's remembering, telling stories with the brain's tongue" and I also feel beholden to "the brain's tongue" — trying to find language for what continually slips from memory, yet insists on its messy present moment anyway. Internal reverie strangles but slides. The momentary um "what my life's become."

Tentacular Thinking

We veer, we slow plan. Our inclinations are rushed, but our savvy is pushed. We shy, we plunge. Our fusion is flexed and the fold we enter into is generous. Randy Lee Cutler writing about the artist Marina Roy says, "These lines form trajectories with a broad reach and tangled implications ensuring that we stay with the trouble, refusing both the nostalgic angling towards an imagined past that never was and the apocalyptic orientation towards a future that may not be, or, at very least, isn't yet." We wander through the thoughts lighting on the articulation of this precise moment. Perpetual patterns quiver leaflike, fossil-centric. We reverberate tangibly. We solidly occupy a lattice one moment before the crumble.

The Art Show

It's good to remember bodies and how they move through the space of the white cube of the Berlinische Galerie via the technological interventions of the 1970s when the work *The Art Show* was conceived. Now the moulded bodies with air-conditioning vents for faces read prophetically via notions of disconnection and mediation. The punch bowl, icon of '70s sociability, is replaced by wine in plastic cups but observations of line and form are similar. Artwork selfies of this artwork keep flashing in the contemporary moment though none of the plastic actors at the time would have had the capacity. Still the self-conscious performance is evident in the placement of plastic bodies in the space of the pretend gallery housed within the real museum. In "Performativity's Social Magic" Judith Butler writes, "The body does not merely act in accordance with certain regularized or ritualized practices, but it *is* this sedimented ritual activity; its action, in this sense, is a kind of incorporated memory." The rituals of viewing in the art show in *The Art Show* are cast and bodies do continue to capitulate. We (in this space) become the memory of the originary performance, the observers of the unseen social/ritual practice, and the makers of the time inbetween.

Zu verschenken

To give away is the infinitive imperative of the gift economy around which arrogance often lurks. "I know what I have given you, but I don't know what you received" is an adage that articulates the space between offer and acceptance. We place a box in a park just down from the low graffitied wall which translates from German roughly to say, "fuck off hipsters" on a board of inexplicable purpose featuring two spray-painted figures seemingly in silent dialogue. We've filled it with the traces of the park, transforming empty sunflower seed wrappers into full bags to maybe induce a sense of wonder like finding a five dollar bill in your winter coat pocket when the season changes. The park is empty, tire swings sizzling in the heat. Down the road a community garden is under threat. When we come back the box is empty but sitting expectantly on the steps. We refill the box and engage in a conversation with a man sitting next to it who generously switches to English.

Unfurl

We were sitting in the classroom in the dark. A woman in our group with long dark hair wanted all the lights out when we played our recording of our assigned text from *The New Long Poem Anthology*. Earlier we had each taken turns reading lines from Daphne Marlatt's "Touch to My Tongue," drinking wine in tiny plastic cups. Our tongues rolled around green flowers and a space opened in my chest, an ache of what I already knew, what we all already know, and a sweet sting of what might be possible. Around 3 a.m. in the poem and in my life at that time, I found my place in language. The lines ran on and could not be contained, a rush I recognized, finally. To arrive at a place you need to know simply where to stop. So I stopped in this text, unfurled a blanket, slid onto my back, and gazed up at its constellations, lulled by the waves when they rolled in, exhilarated by the semantic strikes, the grit behind my eyes.

Yet

Heather gave me her copy of *Touch to My Tongue* after my thesis defense. It was rescheduled so Daphne Marlatt could be my external examiner and Heather got Daphne to sign it for me. The original version with images by Cheryl Sourkes is extremely hard to come by. If there was a fire, I would grab this book. Earlier we interviewed Daphne Marlatt for *filling Station* magazine, a literary publication we all formed during our undergrad. Heather said something like, "I found my place in your writing in the naming of places where I grew up, taking the ferry past Galiano Island, arriving in Victoria," and I said, "I found my place in language here in your poem — finally a way I could write." The only reason I wrote anything was because this book placed me. The way it opened up language to me, the way my body, our bodies could be part of writing. I didn't have to be a disembodied head trapped in rigid lyrical forms or bound to quote clever rhetorical flourishes. That I might be able to articulate something that hasn't been said yet. The form revealing itself, the frame inviting me (in particular) inside.

Eileen Myles

In the dream I phone Eileen Myles because in the dream she posted her number on Instagram and asked people to call. She asks if we've ever slept together and sadly no. It is at this point in the dream that I realize I have nothing to say to Eileen Myles. I think back to a moment at a conference in New York, watching Eileen Myles walk around the place, listening to her talk on a panel with Rae Armantrout, my friend Susan leaning over and whispering, "She's so fucking cool." Back on the phone in the dream I invite her to read at this university. She has read here before and when I went to buy *Inferno* written on the inside cover was "Eileen's copy — do not sell!!" and since I did buy it without knowing that fact, she signs it anyway and it becomes my prized possession until a student borrows it and it's lost.

Furious

Mildly offended or maybe simply jealous that a lovely, super smart poet with an apt name got to write the introduction to the re-released version of Erin Mouré's *Furious*, I still post how excited I am to see the book be made available to another generation of poets. It feels personal. My *Furious* and I remember Erin Mouré saying about Norma Cole's *My Bird Book*, it's MY *My Bird Book* and that's how I know I feel the same. I have said the line "Not act, but act act act" so many times to articulate how time works, what it means in its representation in language, and have mimicked the idea of writing *furiously* like Snoopy on top of his house. Written in the '80s the book still holds up remarkably well, which is exhilarating and also depressing. The idea was for language to change the space (for women) to open it up in language.

Something Quite Peculiar

I met a famous Australian rock star at a poetry festival in Brisbane and the lit conversation over flat whites in the Fortitude Valley street mall perpetuated backstage visits and propelled an insider's perspective on the music industry that was pretty thrilling. My high school boyfriend was a singer in a heavy metal band and one time in Strathmore we had a huge fight when he said he would dedicate a song to me but didn't. "Always Somewhere" is that so hard. Nowadays The Scorpions sound practically poppy. My late-in-life boyfriend was in a band for years and he plays guitar every night but refuses to enact my multi-generational project idea featuring his son and his bandmate's son who are in their own band. He plays reverently now, his fingers burning through all the songs he ever wrote, but only for me. In *How Music Works* David Byrne says, "I resent the implication that I'm less of a musician and a worse person for not appreciating certain works. . . . When I made something, even something crude, I would momentarily discredit and ignore the nagging feeling that said that if I couldn't match the classical or high-quality model then I was somehow less of an artist. My gut was telling me that what I was doing was just fine." My own recent project is to notice how often the thought *you're doing it wrong* arises in my head and to tell that inner voice no, too, to say what I'm doing is *just fine*.

Placebo Effect

filling Station is a literary magazine some university friends and I started in the '90s to bridge aesthetic divides in literary communities as we saw them at the time. We funded early printings with T-shirt and calendar sales and launches with bands in the Republik and the Night Gallery in Calgary. Leslie Feist with the super short '90s style bangs played bass with her band Placebo after the poetry readings. She went to high school with rr who was on the collective and was up for doing us favours. That she became *Feist* and the magazine heads into its 25th year of publishing now are my favourite socio-historical-literary stories. Those perpetual havens still thrive and the return journey home in this poem [*Odyssey*] is its own balm.

NEW NOSTALGIA

"The past has become much more unpredictable than the future."

— Svetlana Boym

What's the matter with you

I remember my back pressed hot into the sandbar one second before my brothers pour water from red buckets onto my tanned belly and I jump up screaming. Exactly one second later I downplay my reaction to not give them the satisfaction. It's a game of pretend I continue for a lifetime. Elif Batuman in *The Idiot* writes, "It can be really exasperating to look back at your past. *What's the matter with you?* I want to ask her, my younger self, shaking her shoulder. If I did that, she would probably cry. Maybe I would cry, too." We regulate our responses to be likeable thereby rendering ourselves weak and undesirable. Only to ourselves, though, only ourselves.

Distrust

We want the girls of our memories to have more agency. To tip our snow globes and rub our rabbit foot key chains until the simple wishes come true. Not the pool-in-the-backyard-winning-the-lottery, but a direct way of being in the world that we could not articulate then and are failing to now. Do you know what we mean? William Gibson in *Distrust That Particular Flavor* writes, "Time moves in one direction, memory in another. We are that strange species that constructs artifacts intended to counter the natural flow of forgetting." What if the can't-be-forgotten event could be re-remembered such that the agency of the scene always shifts to the girl? What if she got what she wanted?

New York Intellectuals

There is a photo of me at 10 wearing a plaid shirt holding up a Bay City Rollers record my sister gave me for Christmas. The boy band with their plaid pant cuffs and their artfully teased hair arranged against the tableau of the Scottish countryside of Leith where they're from. I have hated this photo. My bangs are curled back into an unsuccessful attempt at feathering and they hang in limp chunks. My eyes are huge, my nose red. I have wished to be much cooler, to have my personal history be constructed through better music, more fashionable clothes, cuter style. I have wished the photo would be one of me reading Tolstoy and dressed as a peasant revolutionary or all in black sitting on the steps of a brownstone reading Sylvia Plath like the daughter of feminist New York intellectuals. This is a desire constructed for me by books and also television. D. looking at this exact same photo sees merely an adorable girl. Sara Ahmed writes in *The Promise of Happiness*, "Explanations of relative unhappiness can function to restore the power of an image of the good life in the form of nostalgia or regret for what has been lost" but I wonder if the girl in this photo, instead of being despised for not being worldly enough or glorified as adorable, can simply exist (now) outside of regret?

Video Cameras

In the '90s, when my kids were babies, a friend gave me a video camera that I (secretly) believe she shoplifted. The video camera was subsequently stolen on a family vacation. I admit to being (secretly) relieved and shaped my relief into a new belief system: I would not videotape my kids. I don't know how to explain this decision except in the context of the '90s before everyone had cellphones with cameras. It seemed possible then. My reasoning was that the videos would take over and dominate the memories. Photos give hints at what moments in time might offer, but videos offer too much information. Susan Stewart writes in *On Longing*, "As experience is increasingly mediated and abstracted, the lived relation of the body to the phenomenological world is replaced by a nostalgic myth of contact and presence." Will a generation, growing up with technological records of their growth at every stage, be able to find a tangible connection to the abstract cinematic representation, a twinge in the gut at the sight of videos of them zigzagging on their bike for the first time, a heart rush at the video of digging tiny hands into an entire birthday cake set on a highchair tray? A sticky, hungry, sugar stomach aching, adorable, crying, scared, delighted mélange of feelings that moves us ever closer to every moment we have ever chosen to examine?

Surprise!

I wonder if surprise is still a possibility? A foam snake flinging from a can used to be hilarious, hands over eyes, guess who? or bursts of laughter after someone actually tastes this gross thing. Surprise in the telling of the surprise after that fact. The narrative of surprise. Susan Stewart writes, "Smell and taste lend themselves readily to an aesthetic of surprise and involuntary evocation. . . . Surprise is the result of an unexpected proximity and aggression is linked to repulsion." In the first instance, the sensory reaction calls the memory that feels entirely personal, but the mode of remembering is social and therefore culturally shaped. How we are taught to remember, what memories we have been taught to value, indicates how that memory might feel. The most surprising of recollections are often conjured by smell, a mode of conveyance that bypasses intention. A cupcake might be my madeleine, but I have still always hated surprise parties.

Cognizant

My sister calls in March to say our dad is in the hospital and he can't breathe. I call him on his cellphone and surprisingly he answers, saying, "I'm dying. I'm not kidding," and our goodbye marks the last time I speak to him. I have marked this moment in our life history, have included this detail in a poem I wrote for his memorial service. On the day of his memorial, I decide not to read that part of the poem out loud because it is ours still. His and mine, an intimate moment between us. Later I let that idea go and read the full poem for his interment ceremony. Rebecca Solnit in *The Faraway Nearby* says, "You build yourself out of the materials at hand and those you seek out and choose, you build your beliefs, your alliances, your affections, your home, though some of us have far more latitude than others in all those things." I with a lot of latitude have chosen to build a memory around this event because it's a culturally significant moment, but also because it's a moment of rare intimacy between me and my dad alone, a relationship that is often mediated through my mom, or sisters and brothers. I'm happy for that moment with my dad, painful as it is, but I am also aware that I am my own mediator through this experience. My dad is no longer able to assert his meaning of that last phone call, which might contradict or confirm my own construction. Solnit suggests, "The real question was the caliber of what was mediating experience, and how much you're cognizant of it."

Some Place

I wonder how on Earth this messy "landscape of the present" with its horrifying politics, continual suppression of Indigenous rights, its need for the statement "Black lives matter," its continual brutality toward women and LGBTQ2 people, and its systemic environmental degradation, can be grappled with? Impossible. Is it accurate, I wonder, that until we can (collaboratively, collectively) imagine a progressive future we will remain mired? If we had a way to view the past and the present and the future as not discrete but as interconnected, could we smidgeon a way forward? Kate Eichhorn writes, "Nostalgia is not always about the past; it can be retrospective but also prospective. In fact, we might even think of nostalgia as something that enables the future. When it comes to nostalgia what matters, then, is the context — where we stand in the landscape of the present." I remember reading Kate Millett in the early '90s and writing a paper on my burgeoning (white, so white) feminist consciousness. So many revelations! Seeing the world in a way that finally made sense, but that was also so devastating in its gaps. In her last interview before she died in 2017 Millett said the point was "to get someplace."

Anticipation and Exile

I decided not to make my dad's death public in my social media feeds because my grief felt too intimate, but I also kept revisiting this decision, planning posts with pictures of him in black and white, thinking about what I would say about what he meant to me. I never did make that post, but I'm still thinking about it. If there is nostalgia here, it is for the moment before the tragedy, the desire to go back in time before the loss. Grief is the worst form of longing for a person who can never be returned to. Bronwen Wallace writes "some people are a country / and their deaths displace you. / Everything you shared with them / reminds you of it: part of you in exile / for the rest of your life." I've remembered this line since I heard it in a CanLit poetry class during my undergrad and often pull it out in moments of grief to see if it fits. In some ways, I've kept this line in anticipation of grief. In a more emotionally wrenching kind of way, I have also kept in my mind ways I might survive if anything happened to my adventure-seeking-world-travelling sons: I would scream for days, I would walk through mountains every day for the rest of my life, I would go live in a small village in France where no one knew me and only speak French, I would lie doubled up in pain, I would not be able to make it. When Brennan was younger, he said if anything happened to his brother he would stop talking forever. We anticipate and exile ourselves from grief in whatever ways we can conceptualize.

The Local Exile

My childhood doctor, Dr. Vagyi, escaped to Canada from Hungary after the student-led uprising in 1956, retraining and finally settling in Chase, British Columbia. The story I heard when I was young is that he would fly back to Hungary to visit his mother, but that he could not leave the airport for risk of being arrested. He would fly there, have lunch with his mother, and then fly back. In the moment when airfares were prohibitively expensive and at time when I had never been anywhere on a plane, this was tragic. That he would have to spend so much time and money to travel and only get a few hours with his mom was unbearably sad. In exile, writes Svetlana Boym, "the nostalgic is never a native, but a displaced person who mediates between the local and the universal." In this story, I couldn't reconcile our small town and the vast complexities of a world that would not let a person return home. When I fell off my brother's too-big-for-me golden bike, Dr. Vagyi put five stitches in my knee and told my mom (recovered from fainting at the sight) to buy me a milkshake. Later in his life Dr. Vagyi won the lottery three times and a new skateboard park by Chase Creek was named for him after he died.

Assemblages

The choice to travel results in the production of nostalgia. The arrogance of wanting to belong is a feeling I fight with on every trip I make. Observing the used space of any city is thrilling because the logic of the everyday is continually revealed and utterly visible in a way it often isn't at home. Teju Cole in *Blind Spot* writes, "Assemblages inhabit their own complexity and color. . . . I want to see the things the people who live there see, or at least what they would see after all the performance of tourism has been stripped away. I love these places that are not mine for the underground channel of perception by which they are connected, the common semantics of used space, the shock of familiarity, the impossibility of exact repetition." I do not want to play the role set out for me, do not want to see the moment as fleeting, do not want to experience the painful sting of nostalgia under these circumstances, forgetting (again) that I am the tourist, I am the "performance of tourism."

Recognition Vector

I remember singing "Wish You Were Here" while Nick played guitar in the south of France, the deep intimate conversations I had on the six hour plane ride after my brother's (first) wedding in Hawaii, or talking through the flight from Vancouver to Toronto with someone I'd never see again, like the movie *Lost in Translation* when Bill Murray and Scarlett Johansson talk all night with no implications, each an audience for the other that they'll never have to answer to again, never have to account for, or run into, or explain later. Maybe it's nostalgia for the times when you can be in the moment, time drops away and there is (finally) no need for things to progress, a way to exist outside of belonging. What a relief. This year when I was sitting in a spectacle filled arena listening to a giant screen-projected Roger Waters sing "Wish You Were Here" I cried unexpectedly and then posted the feeling and the photo to Instagram and the moment subsided. Reporting the experience to the group undid the meaning of the original memory, but it also propelled me toward another nostalgic thought, "what a life" (or in the current vernacular #whatislife), as a marker of the time 20s to 50s between my two marked events and locations with that particular song. The transformation of the same old fears. As Maurice Merleau-Ponty suggests, "A preserved fragment of the lived-through past can be at most no more than an occasion for thinking of the past, but it is not the past which is compelling recognition; recognition, when we try to derive it from any content whatever, always precedes itself." A song is a common vector through which to mark a moment, music being a genre we return to in order to understand who we are through the passage of cultural time. "What's the first album you bought?" a common question to determine markers of identity. (For the record, *Eagles Live*. I can still picture the cover and wish it was an edgier choice).

New York Intellectuals II

We grew up in a small town within a tight family, longing for the future in an idyllic place on the shores of the Shuswap Lake. We ran down a long pier and jumped in. We rode our bikes up and down it, barely avoiding careening into tourists there to take a leisurely stroll or take pictures of the surrounding mountain. We drank and smoked pot at the far end of the pier. The cops occasionally moved us along. The air was warm and clear. And we could not wait to leave. We had the longing for uniqueness and our town was always ordinary in our eyes. We used to peruse the ads in the back of the *National Geographic* magazines that our mom subscribed to for educational purposes (remember before the internet) for prep schools, boarding schools. We begged our parents to send us. Which was ridiculous. We lived in a trailer beside the railroad tracks. We were pretty sure we should have been born into a New York intellectual family. Later we do leave, for journalism school and then we leave again for university, and then we leave again to go to school in France, and then again to Montreal. Our parents kept helping us pack and putting us into whatever mode of transportation would get us where we wanted to go. At the same time, our siblings — all smart and perceptive people — moved back home, got jobs, and raised their kids in the place we spent our life trying to escape. The differences in our desires are confusing: "A modern nostalgic can be homesick and sick of home, at once," Svetlana Boym says in *The Future of Nostalgia*.

How Does It Feel

I'm already nostalgic for Patti Smith's Nobel performance, which is the realest thing I've seen in the face of the most ritualistic setting of the contemporary moment. Having the courage to start again, to genuinely state your nervousness, and then to go on and sing Dylan in a more powerfully raw way than Dylan probably could have himself, was incredible to watch because it disrupted the formality of the setting and let her be the most human of humans on the planet. This is "how to be yourself in a performance situation" as the writer Jacob Wren always says. In a *New York Times* article entitled "How Does It Feel," Smith said, "As if in a fairy tale, I stood before the Swedish King and Queen and some of the great minds of the world, armed with a song in which every line encoded the experience and resilience of the poet who penned them." Configuring the setting as a fairy tale evokes a classic form of nostalgia, but the productive usage is the arming of the heroine.

Anticipating Nostalgia

Boyhood — Richard Linklater's 12-year film project — manifests contemporary nostalgia writ large. The film offers clues as to how documentation of everyday life (while drawing attention to its constructedness) could play out for contemporary generations. The star of the film, Ellar Coltrane, says the film changed his perception of reality: "I think the maturation process and the way things change over time and don't change, that's really one of the most striking parts about it is how little anything changes. But that's a very elusive thing. . . . You all look in the mirror, several times a day for most people, and everyone's kind of trying to track how they are changing from day to day much less over a period of years. So to see that all kind of catalogued in front of me [over the course of 12 years] is, very, I don't know, eye opening." One of the functions of nostalgia is to mark out particular moments of time, to make associations with those moments that last over time, and when combining that idea with identity formation his words are telling. We look and look for the change and never see it, looking in the mirror every day and always missing the change. So the "cataloguing" process that we are involved in creates these constructed opportunities to notice change, to see it move before our very eyes. The "elusiveness" that could be attributed to previous generations could be lost when every moment can be called up and replayed. Photographing your face every day for years or the age-your-face apps that give a glimpse into what we might look like in the future, anticipating nostalgia.

Putting the World in a Box

The parts of a whole are indicated in partial modes of remembrances. Loss is a continual gesture of nostalgia. "[Wes] Anderson's films have frequently been compared to the boxed assemblages of Joseph Cornell . . . The box, to Cornell, is a gesture — it draws a boundary around the things it contains, and forces them into a defined relationship," Michael Chabon writes in his introduction to *The Wes Anderson Collection*. If nostalgia is the thing itself, maybe the new nostalgia is the box. The structures are what the new nostalgia is made up of because all the material from the new digitized past can already always be accessed. "Of course the worlds we build out of our store of fragments can be only approximations, partial and inaccurate. As representations of the vanished whole that haunts us, they must be accounted failures. And yet in that very failure, in their gaps and inaccuracies, they may yet be faithful maps, accurate scale models of this beautiful and broken world," Chabon continues. If it is the fragments of impossibility that create the ache, the gathering and boxifying stratifies a future. The way the Anthropocene makes its marks on the parts of our bodies, metallic traces and strange unknown ingestions, the body the box now.

Tender Feelings

"There is a contradiction and naturally returning there comes to be both sides and the center," Gertrude Stein writes in *Tender Buttons*. Gender continuums indicate the contradictory aspect of the body itself. Try to stuff it into a category — mainly one or the other — and people get stuck. We still revel in the category — pretending that it can be meaningful despite shifts in contemporary thinking. A gender reveal party where new parents-to-be give the results of gender tests to a baker who makes a cake that once cut into indicates the corresponding sex organs of the upcoming baby by colour in the usual way — cut through pink and you are about to get a biological girl, blue a biological boy. For the time being. Once the kid appears they will attempt to perform their gender however they want despite social conditioning, all up against the contradiction of parental hopefulness. In a /post-gender/ moment it seems like gender has never mattered more. Judith Butler writes, "To affirm gender diversity is therefore not destructive: it affirms human complexity and creates a space for people to find their own way within this complexity." Like Gertrude Stein's Mrs. Reynolds, we embrace the complexity: "Mrs. Reynolds said she did not mind contradiction, and it was true, she did not, most people do but she did not, it was true, and Mr. Reynolds said it was true when she asked him." We can see the crazy things we're doing, can see the anxious thoughts stirring up and still react in predictable ways. Both sides now. And the fluid center.

Awkward Feelings

Our precipice receptors sting like everyone else's. Like getting mad at our kid for displaying traits we dislike in ourselves. When our kid acts out our worst insecurities, it's okay to stop him! The kid must be strong, must be better, must not make the same mistakes. Must not! Montréal poet Nicole Brossard discusses "le spiral" of time: "When I made the first circle of what would become a spiral, I wanted to illustrate a hole in the patriarchal meaning." To illustrate this hole is to render it graphic: that is, to illuminate it as both written and as vivid, animate — a space for living. Leonard Cohen returning to his Jewish roots at the end of his life, as entrenched as he was in Buddhism. It's not an uncommon phenomenon — the return to the beginning at the end. The nursery rhymes that cycle through Alzheimer's patients and the sweet goodnight. Spiraling through our days. The whoosh of time. The thrill when someone says they thought I was 39 not 49 and how can I be old enough to have a 26-year-old son! I might want to cycle back, but you couldn't pay me to be 13 again. I have awkward feelings about every age I've ever been.

Awkward Writer Feelings

But the idea that someone might find our work in any moment useful for them is pretty compelling, offering a way to understand something that they don't necessarily relate to, or some imaginary future reader coming to work that is formally innovative now, but more mundane in that potential future moment, such that it might transform into a homily, laser stitched onto a future sampler, or discovered and recorded on an EDM track, stuttering and flickering beautifully in future rave scenarios (all would be dreams come true), or even more straightforwardly read as an account of a time, a writer from a small town trying to be taken seriously as an intellectual but always forgetting who to quote off the top of her head, teaching people to write and sometimes, some days, being okay with these roles. Kate Zambreno writes, "I intone to the mirror to myself: You're a fucking genius. Now you try it. The only way our narratives will be told is if we write them ourselves." Our/selves could transform the futures.

Reading

Reading quotes, tweets, snippets. Reading Facebook updates, reading Instagram captions and comments, reading birthday cards (my son makes it a mission to find the most overly sentimental), reading labels, reading receipts, reading recipes. Reading memes. Reading price tags. Reading wedding invitations and instructions. Reading your kid's writing. Reading ingredient lists. Reading menus. Reading prescriptions. Reading scripts. Reading essays, reading creative writing, reading critiques, reading exams, reading reference letters and resumés, reading biographies out loud. Reading reading lists. Reading lists. Reading syllabi. Reading handouts. Reading posters. Reading graffiti. Reading tattoos. Reading links and articles. Reading magazines and newspapers. Reading catalogues. Reading questions. Reading critical theory. Reading reviews. Reading the *Georgia Straight*, the *New York Times*, and the *Guardian* online. Reading headlines. Reading letters. Reading postcards. Reading ad mail. Reading billboards. Reading bills. Reading periods or exclamation points. Reading interrobangs. Reading captions. Reading iBooks. Reading directions and instructions. Reading the weather. Reading the gas gauge. Reading the sign. Reading the room. Reading email and Moodle posts. Reading blogs? Reading comments (don't!). Reading recent calls and text messages. Reading system update requests. Reading emojis. Reading faces. Reading the body.

Mother/hood

It's a trope in contemporary film culture that in scenarios where mothers have sexual relationships after or outside of marriage, something unrelated but bad will happen to their kids. Diane Keaton's role in *The Good Mother*, a film from the '80s, horrified me and probably kept me in my marriage much longer than necessary. Keaton's character, a mother of a young daughter, gets divorced and starts dating. In one scene, her daughter comes into her room while her boyfriend is visiting, she cuddles the young girl in her bed and then carries her back to her room. This scene later becomes the basis for the courtroom justification for the loss of custody of her child. Because her boyfriend was in the room, she was deemed a bad mother, unfit to care for her child. Anyone in a marriage would know that the same scenario, but with a husband, would be seen as normal everyday life. I wish that was the only example. Pity the child characters of mothers who date after marriage because an array of tragedies will befall them. In *Chocolat* while the mother is having sex with Johnny Depp's roguish character, the boat her daughter is staying on almost burns down. I can't watch films with mother characters without cringing in anticipation of the loss.

Momness

Finally, I always appreciate the chance to contemplate the impossible, have considered articulating the unspeakable space that moms take up in formal ways as a continual goal of my practice. Momness is an impossible sense of pushing and being left. My two rubies, les innocents, hold my hand crossing the street in dreams who are impossibly 2 and 22, 7 and 27. Time is absurd if you think of it accreting linearly. Spiralling back embeds its own momentum, throws its own entropy upward.

It Was Meant to Be Simple

It was the book itself and it was trying to put into words how to flourish. Not "how to" exactly but that the act of flourishing might be possible. It was trying to compress language, to say it succinct. It was the way that "photographs create their own memories, and supplant the past." It was the grasp of mirabilia, an apothecary cabinet filled with poetry. How in the photographs of Sally Mann, "there isn't nostalgia for the fleeting moment, captured by chance with a camera. Rather, there's a confession: this moment captured is not a moment stumbled upon and preserved but a moment stolen, plucked from the continuum of experience in order to be preserved." It was holding up those moments, some of which occurred in reading, some of which occurred in life. The moments like a blood-filled heart rushing and pumping like an everyday marvel. Simply a confession that the words, like all experience, exist already but the heart strings still long to be plucked.

FLOURISH: POEMS

"Making a poem is like making a chair; a poem is as real as a chair and sometimes more useful."

— Rebecca Solnit

Seven-Hearted

"I have sung my way through this world"

          — Lorca, "Song of the Seven-Hearted Boy"

it was a feeling of dispersion
it was heavy in the chest
it was part of your body
but it was across the world
beating and moving in Byron Bay
sliding and ripping through Squamish

it was intense and you loved it
trying not to fall into fear

he heard you and he heard you
"I sometimes ran into the wind"
(they both spoke in unison)
and you sent all the power
the love you could find
in each cellular caress
flung it carefully
"in the high mountains"
in the bluegreen seas
to reach the golden eyes
the rich curls

the memories of all the ages
as present as the eternal seconds
of sleepless nights (keep breathing)
a plea or an ultimate encouragement
it was always courage, my love

it was "the hearts that I have"
always a persistent whisper
always keep them safe, keep them safe
keep them safe

the answer cast off
blown back, denser now
carried around
a mirror, a talisman
a crystalized — always —

"Was it you?" — Lorca, "Encounter"

it was meant to be simple
we tried not to hate ourselves

we read "you're a fucking genius"[*] over and over
until it started to stick to the edges of our collective self-doubt

was it you who told me?
"Buried deep in the lyric I lost my mind"[*]

was it you who said,
"I have two selves too"[*]

was it you:
"The one person who does not think I'm nice is me"[*]

you who wrote,
"so you find yourself anywhere"[*]

you said,
"Try, if you can,"[*]

you who insisted,
"Do thine own thing"[*]

---

[*] Kate Zambreno, *Heroines*
[*] Nancy Shaw, *Affordable Tedium*
[*] Kate Zambreno (again)
[*] Heidi Julavits, *The Folded Clock*
[*] Dionne Brand, *Inventory*
[*] Maggie Nelson, *Bluets*
[*] Margaret Christakos, *Her Paraphernalia*

was it you,
"When my life flashes before my eyes, I hope my subconscious turns out to be a skilled curator"*

you, you, you,
"The moments fell open"*

you who suggested,
"feel free"*

---

* Amy Krouse Rosenthal, *Textbook*
* Lorca, "Encounter"
* Zadie Smith, *Feel Free*

Infinity

it was meant to be infinite
la spirale epoch
and we loved
as vastly as we could

it was meant to be perpetual
hand talking our way through days and days
we almost never answered the phone as it rang

we read all the books
losing ourselves in the stacks
shouting "is that all you got"
performing the taunt like dandies
twirling decorative canes
jauntily tossing an opera length glove

we were all the times
all the ages
you were 3 and 23
I was 33 and 53
(and way more)

it all clicked when the tour guide
counted the layers to paradise
in the ceiling of the Alhambra

and remembering my eight-year-old son
saying he'd fly to the moon and wave to me
and now he does, if the moon is whatever continent he's on
and if waving is sending a note on Messenger

we could be in a simulation or
there could be gods of multiple types
time machines might exist
and it's possible that every dog
you ever loved will greet you in heaven
with a big slobbery kiss that never ends

Joy?

"I come to find what I must,
my joy and my identity" — Lorca

it was meant to be simple
we tried to write JOY
and it was simple

dancers rend their heels
into the wood floor of the stage

it was always faces wet with intensity
it was always joy in the midst of deep pain

I try to open myself to catch and not block
so many experiences I have to remind myself
this is for me, I can have this
small town anxieties filter through
you're doing it wrong
my fingers tightly intertwined
I consciously open them palms etched and up
to receive what's on offer —

"the moments fell open & fastened
their roots with my sighs"

is "identity" a trick or a trap
"Life is stronger than
the interpretation of life"
and that felt true last night

I want to stop writing about identity
find a sea green language, a syntax that spurs
gargantuan and garrulous, an epic trail
burgeoning through the green belt
the creek that runs by the mall

"Texts against images and vice versa"*

it was meant to be simple
like teaching the alphabet to a plant*

we repeated our favourite lines over
and over until they divided and multiplied

a clipping, a letter is all there is
at the start of things

a lush touch a rush of fingers entwined
we know it means love in the raw sense
but we reach for the poetic anyway still

all the monkeys in all the rooms
typing on selectrics have not satisfied
our need and this page is just more evidence

we could write all day as the rain pours
diluting our ink to conceptual art levels*

or crystalize pages*
and try to be honest
in the lattice of details
(your warm hand on my belly) (la madre)

and if I sigh deeply it comes from there (her)
and if I howl it comes from there (her) too

---

* *Un Campo Oscuro*, Centro José Guerrero
* John Baldessari, *Teaching a Plant the Alphabet*
* Marcel Broodthaers, *La pluie*
* Greta Alfaro, *Still Life with Books II*

"Texts against images and vice versa" II*

utopia might be signified by tipped letter L
illuminated through weighted 16mm thread*
or nostalgia flipping red and black gestures in ink-on-paper*

or synchronous diving into a green lake
on a heat saturated day, an embodied rush

it might be riding the pain and the flush
of relief on the days your children were born or arrived
in your arms, in your arms

is a long poem long enough to flicker
through desire? (long poem long life)*

volute (n.) a form subsisting in tree bark*
might be enough to show the way

"Let the whole height of the capital be one half
the diameter of the bottom of the column"*
might be a way to calculate spirals of time
to connect us to what we need now

---

* *Un Campo Oscuro*, Centro José Guerrero
* Rosa Barba, *The Long Poem Manipulates Spatial Organization*
* Juan Ramón Jiménez, *Nostalgia*
* Fred Wah, "This Dendrite Map: Father/Mother Haibun"
* Ian Hamilton Finlay, *Seven Definitions Pertaining to the Ideal Landscape*
* Leon Battista Alberti, *De re aedificatoria* quoted in Ian Hamilton Finlay

let watery imperatives sustain themselves
let my son's bus arrive in Arugam Bay
as I walk through the Albaicin
(is the crucial geographical calculation
of this moment but only for us)

Telemachus had a lot to learn about
being a son to a mother who never
wanted to leave home

L. says "everywhere you find a group of men
yelling at a young woman" who devises
a method for staying safe which is part
of conceiving utopia too

"To flourish is to become dangerous" — Robert Frost

it was meant to be simple
resistances were down
we were simply tired

a train arrived and we took it
a bus pulled away from the curb
and then a cab

people were not as trustworthy
as they initially seemed
we grew paranoid and couldn't sleep

drugged to the gills
pushed down hard

it was always Penelope
and rarely Clytaemnestra

it was always waiting up
before settling in
always a shoulder ache
from dreaming about weaving

we wanted to give up jealousy
to be reminded, "other people's
accomplishments don't diminish
our own" to see a counsellor
or psychic who would quietly
say the future is still (somewhat) bright

always a rare glimpse
into the somatic deep
our mind quieting now
our mind rushing away

> "Around the cave/a luscious forest flourished: alder, poplar, and scented cypress. It was full of wings." — *The Odyssey*

it was meant to be simple
we celebrated and it was simple

the details were carefully chosen
wooden vases or mason jars flush with lilacs
candles and particular songs
wine decanters and crystal glasses

it was shoes kicked off
jean jackets over dresses
it was the best that djs could offer

it was awkward at times
someone said no when you
asked them to dance
someone tripped over the lace
edge of their dress someone did
a mock strip tease on a table

sometimes the ache in the chest was full
an emotion like homesickness or a worry
that the love wasn't authentic enough
that it might not hold

it was camping in curling rink
parking lots by the hall so no one
had to drive after

it was a pancake breakfast
the next morning sticky sausages
gluey pancakes it was boyfriends with prosecco
for the orange juice and sisters with baileys
for the coffee and brothers with beer
and clamato juice for the hangovers

it was always, "the rain held off" or
"the dress was gorgeous" always
"all that work" or "so simple and clever"

it was always full
of wings and it always
flourished for a time

" . . . immaculate possibility" — Dionne Brand

it was always rife with possibility
it was always tinged with doubt

historic layers shot through
the architecture's thick walls
statues of the birth of colonialism
willing forth a different answer
when CC reaches his bronzed hand
for money from the queen

(all the ways rewriting can't work)

it was decolonial love*

it was taking down statues
the bricks of residential schools
voices taped on windows and stairwells
#justiceforcolten #justicefortina*

it was territorial acknowledgements
on unceded land

---

* Read *Islands of Decolonial Love* by Leanne Betasamosake Simpson, read *This Wound is a World* by Billy-Ray Belcourt, read *My Conversations with Canadians* by Lee Maracle, read *The Red Files* by Lisa Bird-Wilson, read *The Reconciliation Manifesto* by Arthur Manuel, read *Seven Fallen Feathers* by Tanya Talaga, read *Heart Berries* by Terese Marie Mailhot, read *Elements of Indigenous Style* by Gregory Younging, read *The Marrow Thieves* by Cherie Dimaline, read *As We Have Always Done* by Leanne Betasamosake Simpson, read *X* by Shane Rhodes, read *There There* by Tommy Orange, read *full-metal indigiqueer* by Joshua Whitehead, *This Accident of Being Lost* by Leanne Betasamosake Simpson, read *Moon of the Crusted Snow* by Waubgeshig Rice.
* Site specific artwork by Lacie Burning installed in windows and stairwells at Emily Carr University of Art + Design as part of WRTG/VAST 401, Spring 2018.

sometimes we wanted to rush change
through the pain of unintended consequences
water features and canoes in airports

it was devastating and tragic
it was lonely and awkward

it was powerful in rebellion
set to flourish

"all flourish there, increased by rain" — *The Odyssey*

it was meant to be simple
it rained for days and we loved it
it stopped raining and we missed it

the lilacs bloomed and we rejoiced
stuffing jars and vases
staring longingly out the window
our own *Le Printemps* (1956)
the news tarried beneath

it was always what's the subtext
it was always in the implications

it was always forgetting the umbrella and getting wet
it was always remembering the umbrella and still soaking legs

it was a rhetoric of stupidity
that we always couldn't believe
it was worse than we could've ever imagined
it was porn stars and presidents
it was colonization and erasure
it was rivers and oil companies
it was forests and bulldozers
it was heritage houses and condos

it was always the land
it was always here:
the traditional, ancestral, and unceded territories
of the Musqueam, Squamish, and Tsleil-Waututh First Nations

and always wherever you are
wherever you occupy

Flourish

"Avoid the flourish" — Leonard Cohen, "How to Speak Poetry"

it was meant to be simple
we loved it and it was simple
a plain pine box
as hearts broke
to cries of hallelujah

it was meant to be
simple
it was meant
to be
it was
meant

it had meaning
the people agree
as they post versions of "Hallelujah"
as others post telling them
they are posting the wrong
"Hallelujahs"

a fight broke out
about who "Famous Blue Raincoat"
meant more to
nostalgia for a lost love
or whisper-singing in bed
as a sign of contemporary intimacy
who soothes your insomnia at "4 in the morning/the end of December"?

it was a gravel voice, a gravelly voice
it was profound and it sang out to the hills
it was always a hymn, it was always an anthem
it went "a thousand kisses deep" or it broke open
"the crack to let the light in"

it was many things
to many people
it was always a dance, always a poem
always thinly veiled fiction
it was beautiful and it was loser-ish
it was mine more than yours
yours more than mine

it was trouble for a troubled time
it was humility in the crease of greatness
it was always an epic, an ode
it made you cry every time
it unleashed you, untethered
it made you freer, it let you off
your flight, light, bright
it was always surrender
it was always trying to figure you out
it was always helping you, giving you courage
it was fragments and pieces, it was notions
it was always deep understanding
it was eventually

it was soft and you loved it
it was always from a distance
it was always "you look good when you're tired"
always "you look like you could go on forever."

Pavilion

(for Roy)

> "Sweet bluebells used to flourish there
> And tall trees waved on high,
> And through their ever sounding leaves
> The soft wind used to sigh."
>
> — "Alexander and Zenobia," Anne Brontë

it was meant to be simple
soliphilia for a new age
smoky or floating in green
held like whatever tempts
in waves blown back not
salty not arid not acrid nor
bleak in any way

i want to say verdant, so
what? lush and lit up

it was meant to be peaceful
to harbour calm it was meant
to be fun, an adventure

it was many things to
a family of people
many people whose joy
would not be the same
without its many things

it was always long conversations
books on the dock it was always
diving or swimming, fishing or
floating, it was wind slippering
through birch leaves or blue jays
percolating a monochromatic vision

it was hot and we loved it
it was always nocturne and moonlit
it was always lacustrine and lovely
ecological and efferent
adorned by microbialites
it was a contemporary wonder
and studied by astronauts

it was nails and building
fixing and maintaining
leaves and burning
it was travail collectif
w/ beer or bourbon

it was the new nostalgia
made manifest

framed photo collages
crib board w/ matchstick markers
scrabble with two incomplete sets
of letters

"The past . . . much more
unpredictable than the future"

it was a million moments
to grasp glittering on return

it was this poem: a wet bathing suit
peeled off at the end of the day

Quietly

"Change the oil when the light comes on" — My dad

it was meant to be simple
we loved it and it was simple
a plain pine box as
at least six hearts broke

on the phone he told me, "I'm dying
I'm not kidding" and I appreciated
the chance to say goodbye

"when people show you who
they are, believe them"

that morning my mom described
him as actions-over-words, one rose
dried beautifully for every year

what passes for love is simple
you come home and he fills your
car with gas, makes you coffee
in the morning, drives you to the
airport so early you could never miss
a flight

what is love, is simple
we loved him and it was simple
not always easy, but basic
at the heart of things

I remember his hand on the back of
my bike seat running,
one push to let go
and I was free, pedalling
toward the weeping willow
on my own power
and he was simply
standing there
light plaid shirt
arms folded and proud

it was memory and it was forgetting
a million moments that passed for him
that we can't know

it was bringing home fried chicken
or making beef stew for dinner on Friday nights

making fudge we could never wait to set
eating it with spoons crowded in the kitchen

it was always home and always familiar
always building and fixing his own way
always self-taught and interested always
ready for a conversation leaping ahead

it was safe and you loved it
you could always go back

it was love and he loved us
quietly, but deeply

loving our own children is easy
like breathing
letting go is hard
but we ride the wave of their exhilaration
arms folded and proud

The Drink

it was meant to be simple
we drank it in and it was simple

it was always what we could abide
versus what got us up in arms
always where we sent our money
versus where we were reluctant to click

it was how many before bed
or glasses of wine before dinner
it was crisp and we loved it
it was messy and we hated it

our cultural theory heroines
embossed on candles or cards
depicted as plastic action figures

it was simply quitting with no fanfare
or it was excessive and blurry

we said the wrong things
always the things we were thinking
and should never out loud

always the things we were thinking
circling fear at 3 a.m. shame 'til 5
and finally a ragged sleep

it was always repetitive
always tinged with dangerous edges
even if mornings were bright

it was always open arms
always the love flowed
and pummelled like wine

The Work

it was meant to be simple
a pedagogical concept
centred around collaboration

it was always, "how can we get
them to" and "what can we
reasonably expect"

it was how many pages
and the length of essays
always reflection turned to numbers
numbers turned to letters

it was course evals and
conference papers
always peer reviews
and workshops

it was meetings and committees
always "don't do too much
work" versus feeling like
it was a good job
always one more email
before the end of the day

Proposals

it was meant to be simple
one ring of enthusiasm
to indicate the connection

it was meant to be phrased
as a question not reluctantly
but with all the love you had
have. all the love you do have

it was indicative of a tension
or a desire that rose so high
it couldn't be contained

sometimes it was staged elaborately
in hot-air balloons or the intermissions
of sporting events, sometimes it
couldn't possibly go over
the awkwardness almost unbearable

sometimes the yes was so enthusiastic
the questioner doubted their intention
sometimes the ring was returned
and had to be remade, its symbolic
value too weighty to be worn again

sometimes it meant something for a while
and then changed to mean nothing at all

FLOURISH: DECLARATIVE SENTENCES

"[The] elegiac tends to be something like the absence of a landscape, the absence of a place, the determination to let one's life fall and rise upon love itself, and love itself then bringing an order that passes all the time. . . .

"I see what enormous intelligence that nostalgia has because what it does is throw all of us . . . into the realm of . . . actual grief and tears of the modern condition."

— Robin Blaser,
The Astonishment Tapes

Dear

"In that vague, formative past, love was written with a flourish, and it flourished" — Lynne Tillman*

(I) feathered my hair, never perfectly, arc of tresses front to back.

Photos (selfies) always show a gap, a place where I/you/we don't appear.

How much (I) wish to charge up the details, construct an intellectual life story.

How much (you) love the stories you have, diving in over and over.

Dear is a trustworthy opening, a normative plea; a tree (we) love.

(all the calm space, loyalty as deep green as a lake)

Opening belies shame; a sweet release from vague weights.

Polishing disillusions doesn't get us far so dear one (we) jump.

Asynchronous fluidity is ours (again?) (we) float for so long.

When heat burns (we) scratch sunscreen into our backs.

Lingering is our currency and (we) fight for it.

One leaf or two weighs us down lightly.

---

* "Love melts 'you' into 'I' or is it just grammar that bends 'I' into 'you,' just that old subject to object-of-the-verb magic? Love dissolves disbelief, since it defies credulity. Love establishes an impossible, enduring, tender, spidery bridge between us, two poor pronouns. You and I are simple, one-word syllable words, you and I need love."

Absence

Ledgers make light of the news.

Policy equates practice, designates who is who.

You book it, reveal the power where light might leak.

All thorough, a pencil erases tremulous views.

Numbers can dictate geography, as well as balances.

(all the ways I inhabit you, take you in)

Rain evaporates eventually and it gets too hot to sleep.

Volumes of Stein riffling in the wind left open.

You can't survive without guts, gutters.

A return clunks if a typewriter, or if a driveway full of parked cars.

Ivy covers. Love persists.

Presence

Erudite licks embossed dictionary covers methodically.

Rain is not gold, nor the colour of truth; merely green in essence.

Subtext is always the opposite of pretense; underneath a scream.

Laughter ticks proprioceptively especially under soft covers.

Clouds can be beds or imaginary pillows as well as dewy cells.

(all this and your skin in the morning)

Lingual utterance is another way of saying the weather or love.

Euphoria kicks forth beneath a skylight with some force.

Conjurers make the illusory tangible, a confidence man too.

Ether settles in, says come to me insistently.

Distill an ellipsis (wait) it rains.

Presents

There are no cards to fit the occasion.

It is a long time and it glimmers like fingernails in dish soap.

Persistence is a virtue, as well as a vice.

Flotsam caught in a slipstream just keeps moving.

Time is mostly unmarked, unaccounted for moment-by-moment.

(all the shores you have washed up on)

Swimming can be chlorinated or full of gold mica specks.

Magical is in the inference, the shaping of the narrative.

Some stories are painful, some delightful.

Repetition cries out for more of the same, luxuriates in the familiar.

More of the same. Tissue paper falls delicately or crumpled.

Light Light

Lustre is remarkable, says look at me longer.

Pay attention, are you listening to what I'm saying?

Hips make meaning emphatic whether swish or click.

Birthdays easily forgotten, unremarked even on Facebook.

Mail slurps up its undeliverable packages.

(all the days you can possibly remember)

Shopping can frustrate as well as enlighten.

Stores produce excess, of course.

Privilege screams about too much choice always.

Abject writes narratives about domestic scenarios.

If you can't find what you like, look up.

Best

Summer dives into a green lake synchronically.

Light buoys structures, whether docks or poems.

Heat penetrates beach towels, backs.

Driftwood big enough to sit on, a makeshift hammock.

Beer with lime is a crisp surrender.

(my generative grammar washes over your prescriptive grammar)

Sand can be gritty, but also cold packed underfoot.

Waves like ruffles from shore, like bumping into barrels on the boat.

Weeds could pull you under, but swim anyway.

Motivation works better outside of self-help books, TED Talks.

Questions disguised as short (but lyrical) speeches.

How much we want this to work. Aquamarine shimmer in the lens.

Volute

Spirals wander through oceans, flash in the minds of writers as concepts.*

Time as a spiral is way better than time as a bullet (that's obvious).

The frame of a poem is "a space for living."

Beside the advice: don't write about writing.

Water is a container for plastic, as much as a sparkly metaphor.

(We float through the saddest thing we've ever seen).

Illumination is aquamarine breath, ripe in the lungs.

If a damp settles in our syntax gets sandy, grit behind the eyes.

A whorl is a way.

Scraping through discomfort, a bladed implement.

A rhetoric of perpetual apologies.

---

* Nicole Brossard says, "'When I made the first circle of what would become a spiral, I wanted to illustrate a hole in the patriarchal meaning.' To illustrate this hole is to render it graphic: that is, to illuminate it as both written and as vivid, animate — a space for living."

Tremour

When we feel it, we know. A text pings or an alarm sounds.

Lemons know how to be squeezed. Limes too. Garlic gets crushed.

We love in lattices, bright patterns, resist rendering the divine.

Monogamy won't be forced but we're free to choose it.

Traction can be gained. With or without our fervour.

(all the ways I miss you, sharp acid on the tongue)

A lake will always ripple when we enter.

Shock of cold is good for us.

Hot flashes are luxurious, but also oppressive, weighty.

Wood slivers, wool caresses. Both can be itchy.

We feel what we now know.

Lights linger up the snowdrifts.

The book itself

was a list of names, places, types
the type was mixed up and reordered constantly
constancy was a value being promoted
promos for the author were interspersed
interspersion shot forth like a canon
canonical asses were sprayed for once
once was not even the first word
words piled up beautifully like Stein
Stein never loved Picasso obviously
obvious overtones swung like pendulums
pendulum would make a great swing, my son said
saying it with small voice whispering *pendulum pendulum*
pendulum momentum shifts are epic rafters
rafters trip up earthquake zones you should pay
pay more attention to preparation and frantically undo
undo the more tragic consequences was the book
bookish enough to be about that particular apocalypse
apocalypse's imaginary friend, hey Oller
Oller buddy what do you see from the other side?

siding with the others in your fit fabula
fabulously rendered as always
always you with a pen in your hand
hands frantically waving the keys
keys gangling back up to reach you
you with text embedded in your print creases
creases for days my love intense — you wouldn't call them poems —
poems maybe no, but bright messages fingery puppets
puppets perceptively applied for maximum frivolity
frivolity in the contemporary sense meaning still pretty serious

seriously playing to the crowd now
now you sense the fine movement
movements shift to acquire
acquire your lightness
lightness of being
being you stole

ACKNOWLEDGEMENTS

Thank you to Michael Holmes and everyone at ECW Press. Our 20-year working relationship is one of the great triumphs of my life. Thank you to copy editor extraordinaire Emily Schultz. (If you haven't read her work go do that right now.) Thank you to Cybèle Creery and Shane Rhodes for their readings and responses to this project and more importantly for their friendship from the '90s *filling Station* days to now. Thank you (always) to Meredith Quartermain and Nicole Markotic. Thank you to Gerry Shikatani, Lisa Bird-Wilson and Fiona Tinwei Lam for insights in Granada. Thank you to Susanne Bosch and Paz Ponce for creating collaborative potentials in Berlin. Thank you to the Canada Council for the Arts for supporting these residencies. Thank you to my colleagues and students at Emily Carr University of Art + Design, especially Heather Fitzgerald and everyone in the Writing Centre + the Aboriginal Gathering Place. It's a pleasure to work among writers + artists + friends every single day. Thank you to the Coast Salish people: the Musqueam, Squamish, and Tsleil-Waututh First Nations on whose unceded traditional territories this work was written and to the Secwepemc people from where I grew up. Thank you to my son Brennan and my son Blake, each for the delights of adventures they continue to share with me all over the world. Having children who are explorers and seekers is the great joy of my life, but if either of you is reading this, call home more. Thank you to Mum and my family in Chase, which continues to grow into the next generations. You all make me proud. Thank you to the Karjalas one-and-all, but especially Damon. This book is for my dad.

NOTES

FLOURISH: STUDIES

Beauty will no longer be forbidden
Medusa mosaic, Mosque-Cathedral of Córdoba
Hélène Cixous, "The Laugh of the Medusa," *Signs*, vol. 1, no. 4, Summer, 1976, pp. 875–893.
Adrienne Rich, *Snapshots of a Daughter-in-Law*, W.W. Norton & Company, 1967.

Lost in Translation
Jhumpa Lahiri, *In Other Words*, Knopf, 2016.

The Inbetweenists
Heidi Julavits, *The Folded Clock*, Bloomsbury, 2017.
Lucian Freud, *Last Portrait* (1976–1977), Museo Nacional Thyssen-Bornemisza, Madrid.

Buttons and Pockets
Harryette Mullen, *Trimmings*, Tender Buttons, 1991.
Misha Glouberman and Sheila Heti, *The Chairs Are Where the People Go*, Farrar, Straus and Giroux, 2011. The exercise discussed in this poem is a variation on "The Rocks Game." Thanks to Matt Rader for pointing it out and for the adaptation from rocks to buttons.

Una Habitación Propia
Virginia Woolf, *A Room of One's Own*, Harvest Book, 2005.
Andrés Soria Olmedo, *Una Habitación Propia: Federico García Lorca en la residencia des estudiantes, 1919–1936*, Centro Federico García Lorca, Granada, 2018.

Lorca's Piano
The Fiona in this poem is the poet Fiona Tinwei Lam. Please read her work: *Enter the Chrysanthemum*, Caitlin Press, 2009; *Intimate Distances*, Nightwood Editions, 2002; and the many wonderful anthologies she has edited.

Centro José Guerrero
James Elkins, *Pictures & Tears: A History of People Who Have Cried in Front of Paintings*, Routledge, 2004.

Façadism
Jane Jacobs, *The Death and Life of Great American Cities*, Vintage, 1961.
Vancouver Art Gallery Façade Festival, 2017. facadefest.com

La Lectura
Aline Masson Raimundo de Madrazo y Garreta, *La Lectura*, Museo Carmen Thyssen, Malaga.
Jason Gots, "Karl Ove Knausgaard — The Way I Should Be in the World," *Think Again Podcast* #132, January 26, 2018.

Tout Va Bien
Jean-Michel Alberola, *Vouz avez le bonjour de Marcel*, 2002, Centre Pompidou, Malaga.
Sara Ahmed, *The Promise of Happiness*, Duke University Press, 2010. I found this book on a library shelving cart while I was waiting to talk to my librarian friend and it has proved invaluable. Such sweet serendipity!

Sketch of the Poem of Cordoba
Julio Romero de Torres, *Sketch of the Poem of Cordoba*, Museo Carmen Thyssen, Malaga.

Etel Adnan, "To Write in a Foreign Language," *An Etel Adnan Reader*, Nightboat Books, 2014.

Hullo, Hullo . . . ,

Women to Watch, National Museum of Women in the Arts, Washington, D.C., 2010.

Lynne Tillman, "Beginning Middle End," *Frieze*, December 19, 2017.

Rose Wylie, *Hullo, Hullo*, Centro de Arte Contemporaneo de Malaga.

La Vega

Sana Elouazi, "Spain to Hire 7,000 Moroccan Farm Workers for 2018," *Morocco World News*, December 12, 2017, moroccoworldnews.com/2017/12/236207/spain-hire-7000-moroccan-farm-workers-2018. (Thanks to Fiona Tinwei Lam for this link.)

Tokyo Cool

Banana Yoshimoto, *Moshi Moshi,* Counterpoint, 2016.

Ali Smith, *Artful,* Hamish Hamilton, 2013.

Masterpieces

Vincent van Gogh, *Les Vessenots in Auvers*, 1890, Museo Nacional Thyssen-Bornemisza, Madrid.

An H in the Heart

Roy Kiyooka, *Strang*, 1963, Art Gallery of Ontario.

Cam Scott (@vanishingsigns), Twitter.

bpNichol, *An H in the Heart*, McClelland & Stewart, 1994.

You Don't Know How Lovely You Are

Camilla Ackley, *Into the Fold* intothefoldmag.com.

Adrian Searle, "Gillian Wearing takeover: behind the mask — the Self Portraits," *The Guardian*, 2012.

Jacqueline Turner, *Into the Fold*, ECW Press, 2000.

Speaking in Paragraphs
bpNichol, *Selected Organs*, Black Moss Press, 1988.

Tentacular Thinking
Randy Lee Cutler, "Folding the Longue Durée into Deep Time: Marina Roy's Entangled Worlds," *BlackFlash* 35.1, April 2018.

The Art Show
Edward Kienholz and Nancy Reddin Kienholz, *The Art Show*, Berlinische Galerie, Berlin.

Judith Butler, "Performativity's Social Magic," in *Bourdieu: A critical reader*, Blackwell, 1999.

Zu verschenken
The park is in Neukölln, Berlin.

Prachttomate is a community garden under threat: prachttomate.de.

This site-specific project was conceived with Felix Classen, Natalia Masewicz, and William Smith as part of the Affect: Tools for Conviviality residency at Agora Collective in Berlin, July 2018.

Unfurl
Sharon Thesen, ed. *The New Long Poem Anthology*, Coach House Press, 1991.

Yet
Daphne Marlatt, *Touch to My Tongue*, Longspoon, 1984.

"Daphne Marlatt Taken in(side) — interview," *filling Station*, 13.

Eileen Myles
Eileen Myles, *Inferno (a poet's novel)*, OR Books, 2010.

Update: After writing this poem, the book reappeared! It is once again among my prized if-there-was-a-fire-I'd-grab-it possessions.

Furious
Erin Mouré, *Furious*, House of Anansi, 1988.

Erin Mouré, *Furious*, Introduction by Sonnet L'Abbé, House of Anansi, 2018.

Something Quite Peculiar
David Byrne, *How Music Works*, McSweeney's, 2012.

Placebo Effect
filling Station Magazine: fillingstation.ca

Emily Wilson, translator, Homer *The Odyssey*, W.W. Norton & Company, 2018.

NEW NOSTALGIA

What's the matter with you
Elif Batuman, *The Idiot*, Penguin Books, 2017.

Distrust
William Gibson, *Distrust That Particular Flavor*, Putnam, 2012.

New York Intellectuals
Sara Ahmed, *The Promise of Happiness*, Duke University Press, 2010.

Video Cameras
Susan Stewart, *On Longing*, Duke University Press, 1993.

Surprise!
Susan Stewart, *Poetry and the Fate of the Senses*, University of Chicago Press, 2001.

Cognizant
Rebecca Solnit, *The Faraway Nearby*, Penguin, 2013.

Some Place
Kate Eichhorn, "Feminism's There: On Post-ness and Nostalgia," *Feminist Theory*, October 2015.
Kate Millett, *Sexual Politics*, Columbia University Press, 1970.
Rachel Shteir, "A Last Interview with Kate Millett," *The New Yorker*, September 13, 2017.

Anticipation and Exile
Bronwen Wallace, *Common Magic*, Oberon Press, 1985.

The Local Exile
Svetlana Boym, *The Future of Nostalgia*, Basic Books, 2001.
Emily Wilson, translator, Homer, *The Odyssey*, W.W. Norton & Company, 2018.

Assemblages
Teju Cole, *Blind Spot*, Random House, 2017.

Recognition Vector
Maurice Merleau-Ponty, *Phenomenology of Perception*, Routledge & Kegan Paul, 1974.

New York Intellectuals II
Svetlana Boym, *The Future of Nostalgia*, Basic Books, 2001.

How Does It Feel
Jacob Wren, *Authenticity is a Feeling*, Book*hug, 2018.
Patti Smith, "How Does It Feel," *The New Yorker*, December 14, 2016.

Anticipating Nostalgia
Promotion for the film even included a "nostalgia generator": boyhoodnostalgia.com
Esther Zuckerman, "Talking About the Nostalgia of 'Boyhood' with its Star, Ellar Coltrane" *The Wire*, July 10, 2014.

Putting the World in a Box
Matt Zoller Seitz, Introduction by Michael Chabon, *The Wes Anderson Collection*, Abrams Books, 2013.

Tender Feelings
Gertrude Stein, *Three Lives & Tender Buttons*, Signet Classics, 2003.
Judith Butler, "The backlash against 'gender ideology' must stop," *New Statesman*, January 2019.
Gertrude Stein, *Mrs. Reynolds*, Sun & Moon Press, 1988.

Awkward Feelings
Nicole Brossard, Judith Roof, and Melissa Bailar, "An Interview with Nicole Brossard," Johns Hopkins University Press, 2016.

Awkward Writer Feelings
Kate Zambreno, *Heroines*, Semiotext(e), 2012.

It Was Meant to Be Simple
Valeria Luiselli, *Lost Children Archive*, Alfred A. Knopf, 2019.

FLOURISH: POEMS

Seven-Hearted
Federico García Lorca, "Song of the Seven-Hearted Boy."

"Was it you?"
Federico García Lorca, "Encounter."
Kate Zambreno, *Heroines*, Semiotext(e), 2012.
Nancy Shaw, *Affordable Tedium*, Tsunami Editions, 1987.
Kate Zambreno (again), *Heroines*, Semiotext(e), 2012.
Heidi Julavits, *The Folded Clock*, Bloomsbury, 2017.
Dionne Brand, *Inventory*, McClelland & Stewart, 2006.
Maggie Nelson, *Bluets*, Wave Books, 2009.
Margaret Christakos, *Her Paraphernalia*, Book*hug, 2016.
Amy Krouse Rosenthal, *Textbook*, Dutton, 2016.
Federico García Lorca, "Encounter."
Zadie Smith, *Feel Free*, Hamish Hamilton, 2018.

Joy?
Federico García Lorca, "I come to find what I must, my joy and my identity," "Encounter."
Carolivia Herron, *Thereafter Johnnie*, 1st Books, 2001. With thanks to Jacob Wren's Twitter feed for this quote.

"Texts against images and vice versa"
Un Campo Oscuro at Centro José Guerrero, Granada, 2018.
John Baldessari, *Teaching a Plant the Alphabet*.
Marcel Broodthaers, *La pluie*.
Greta Alfaro, *Still Life with Books II*.

"Texts against images and vice versa" II
Un Campo Oscuro at Centro José Guerrero, Granada, 2018.

Rosa Barba, *The Long Poem Manipulates Spatial Organization.*

Juan Ramón Jiménez, *Nostalgia.*

Fred Wah, "This Dendrite Map: Father/Mother Haibun," *The New Long Poem Anthology*, 2001.

Ian Hamilton Finlay, *Seven Definitions Pertaining to the Ideal Landscape.*

Leon Battista Alberti, De re aedificatoria quoted in Ian Hamilton Finlay, *Seven Definitions Pertaining to the Ideal Landscape.*

L is Lisa Bird-Wilson. Read her books *Just Pretending* from Coteau Books, 2013, and *The Red Files* from Nightwood Editions, 2016.

"Around the cave
a luscious forest flourished: alder, poplar,
and scented cypress. It was full of wings."

Emily Wilson, translator, Homer, *The Odyssey*, (5. 63–64), W.W. Norton & Company, 2018.

". . . immaculate possibility"

Dionne Brand, *Inventory*, McClelland & Stewart, 2006.

Leanne Betasamosake Simpson, *Islands of Decolonial Love*, ARP Books, 2013.

Billy-Ray Belcourt, *This Wound is a World*, Frontenac House, 2017.

Lee Maracle, *My Conversations with Canadians*, Book*hug, 2017.

Lisa Bird-Wilson, *The Red Files*, Nightwood Editions, 2016.

Arthur Manuel, *The Reconciliation Manifesto*, Lorimer, 2017.

Tanya Talaga, *Seven Fallen Feathers*, House of Anansi, 2017.

Terese Marie Mailhot, *Heart Berries*, Penguin Random House, 2018.

Gregory Younging, *Elements of Indigenous Style*, Brush Education, 2018.

Cherie Dimaline, *The Marrow Thieves*, Dancing Cat Books, 2017.

Leanne Betasamosake Simpson, *As We Have Always Done*, University of Minnesota Press, 2017.

Shane Rhodes, *X*, blewointment, 2013.

Tommy Orange, *There There*, Penguin Random House, 2018.

Joshua Whitehead, *full-metal indigiqueer*, Talonbooks, 2017.

Leanne Betasamosake Simpson, *This Accident of Being Lost*, House of Anansi, 2017.

Waubgeshig Rice, *Moon of the Crusted Snow*, ECW Press, 2018.

Art installation by Lacie Burning at Emily Carr University of Art + Design, part of WRTG/VAST 401, Spring 2018. Check out their powerful curatorial and installation work: burning.live

"all flourish there, increased by rain"

Emily Wilson, translator, Homer, *The Odyssey* (9.111), W.W. Norton & Company, 2018.

Flourish

Leonard Cohen, "How to Speak Poetry," *Stranger Music*, McClelland & Stewart, 1993.

Pavilion

Anne Brontë, *Self Communion/Alexander and Zenobia*, CreateSpace Publishing, 2016.

Svetlana Boym, *The Future of Nostalgia*, Basic Books, 2001.

FLOURISH: DECLARATIVE SENTENCES

Robin Blaser, *The Astonishment Tapes: Talks on Poetry and Autobiography with Robin Blaser and Friends*, Miriam Nichols, ed., The University of Alabama Press, 2015. With thanks to Meredith Quartermain for unearthing this Blaser treasure, which deepened my understanding of this project.

Dear

Lynne Tillman, *The Complete Madame Realism and Other Stories*, Semiotext(e), 2016.

Volute

Nicole Brossard, Judith Roof, and Melissa Bailar, "An Interview with Nicole Brossard," Johns Hopkins University Press, 2016.